Fairy Tale and Nursery Rhyme Mysteries

The story behind the rhymes.

A text without context is a pretext.

Knox Chamblin

What really happened with Jack and Jill

We were told that Jack and Jill went up a hill to get some water. However, a tragic accident occurred that Jack fell down the hill and cracked his skull. Soon Jill came tumbling after. She came away unhurt. Jill hesitated to call for help for at least an hour. Why? Why couldn't they have gotten water from the pump outside their home? So, did Jill push Jack down the hill because of some unknown argument? Was there someone else at the well? What do we really know about Jack and Jill.

The hill in question was not steep enough to cause Jack to fall, so did he trip on a rock? His pail was empty and it is believed he never got a chance to get any water. Jill claimed it was an accident, but then why did she fall landing unscathed at the bottom of the hill? Did she need an alibi? The parents sent their teenagers because the buckets would have been heavy full of water. The story didn't tell us if they were brother and sister? Neighbors? Why send both?

It was later found that Jack had a crush on Jill, but she had a boyfriend named Butch. Did the boyfriend push both of them down the hill? Did Jill lie to protect her boyfriend? On the hillside there were no rocks, so how did he break his crown on a hill with only a twenty degree slope? No weapon was found to cause the wounds on his head other than a possible fall.

Jack, also known as the night crawler, was being watched by the police thinking he was the one wandering around in the middle of the night peering in windows. Could there have been an irate neighbor that took his revenge on Jack, but why didn't Jill say something?

There were many questions that needed to be answered. Jack couldn't give his side of the story as he lay in a coma for days on end. When he finally awakened he had no memory of the incident. An addition to the story years later had Jack recovering and Jill got only a spanking which was far from the truth. The town didn't want the real story to get out so they made up their own legend.

Police investigated the incident and Jill's conflicting stories of the event led to her arrest for assault and attempted murder. In court she claimed self-defense. However, Jack was unable to testify as he succumbed to be essentially a vegetable to this day. The jury did not believe her and the judge gave her 5-10 years in prison. As she was taken from the courtroom she exclaimed "But he tried to kiss me!"

After serving three years she was released and later arrested for prostitution in New York City. Jack ended up a hopeless vegetable living with his parents.

News update: Simple Simon did meet a pie man, but had no money to pay for the pies. When the pie man refused to let him have a taste, Simple Simon pulled out a gun and stole all the pie man's wares. It only took a matter of hours to find Simple Simon in a local clinic complaining of stomach pains. After being arrested, the judge found him being too simple and allowed him to be free. He was escorted home and his parents were allowed to watch over him.

The mystery behind the death of Humpty Dumpty

Was Humpty Dumpty's death a case of murder? Accident? Suicide? This was a strange case since there were many witnesses and no one agreeing to what they saw. Humpty's brother, Dumbty, was seen fleeing the scene soon after his brother fell. Did Dumbty intentionally push Humpty off the wall in some sibling rivalry fit of anger? Or was Dumbty afraid of the King's men who were camped nearby.

The King's men were close by with their rations low and little to eat. Did they prod Humpty to the ground for one good omelet? The Captain of the King's men protested that his men had nothing to do with the fall. However, the Captain exonerated his men, not himself. Why were the King's men so concerned to put Humpty Dumpty together again? Why was Humpty so important?

Why after years of wall sitting did Humpty happen to fall at that time and place? These are questions to be asked and answered. Why was Humpty on the wall in the first place? He sat silently staring into the distance for days at a time. He never read a book to pass the time. Was he spying on someone? Was he working as a spy for the King's men or was he a traitor which is why the King's men might have knocked him off the wall?

When questioned about the yoke of Humpty, the Captain said: "It must've seeped into the ground." Having no evidence of any other possibility there was nothing that could be done. Was it an effort to get rid of the evidence that Humpty was a bad egg? Some of the King's men did have food poisoning some time afterward.

Was Humpty suicidal? To deepen the mystery Humpty's brother Dumbty claimed his brother was depressed. His mother disagreed.

Their father had no comment except to say "If I say anything I'll probably end up with egg on my face." Investigators saw nothing funny about the incident.

    The investigation still continues with Humpty's friends, but without witnesses to verify anything had happened nothing can be resolved. All that is left is an empty shell and a hollow story of death by unknown means.

News update: Mary had a little lamb……nuff said.

Jack Spratt and his wife found dead in their home.

It was gleaned from the autopsy report that Jack died of starvation. His wife died of a massive heart attack. Murder-suicide? Neighbors heard the Spratts arguing in the last few weeks before their death. Jack refused to eat any fat, anything with cholesterol, or food additives. His wife ate just about anything though her doctor warned her of possible heart problems.

Jack walked with two canes and looked emaciated according to his neighbors. His boss said he had not seen Jack for two days before his death. Witnesses said that Mrs. Spratt sat outside in her garden eating pies and cakes while shaded with a massive umbrella.

When Jack had a nasty fall in his garden while trying to pick one of his roses. Mrs. Spratt never stirred from her chair except to give Mr. Spratt a withering stare. Their neighbors watched as she finally said to Mr. Spratt, "Get up, you lazy fool before the neighbors see you."

Jack mumbled something to which Mrs. Spratt replied "If I go, you go, too!" Extremely annoyed Mrs. Spratt struggled to get up and approached Jack. The neighbors continued by telling the police how she picked up Jack's limp body and went into the house. They heard a loud moan after the Spratt's were inside. It was then the neighbors called the police.

The police entered the house of the Spratt's and found them both dead on the floor with Mrs. Spratt sprawled on top of her husband. Was it intentional? Autopsy showed that Mr. Spratt's ribs were crushed and a lung collapsed which caused his death. Mrs. Spratt had a massive coronary. The case is still under investigation.

Jack of Jack be nimble fame found burned to death

Family members found the sixty-five year old Jack burned to death in his back yard. The elderly Jack was unable to jump over one last candlestick. The compulsive candle stick jumper risked life and limb by insisting the candles be lit before he jumped over them. He made enough money over the years so that he could build his own candle factory. His ashes will be scattered near the candle factory he ran for forty years. It was estimated that fifty mourners came to the funeral holding lit candles as a tribute to Jack.

Eulogy: Jack neither was nimble nor as quick when last he jumped almost over his last candlestick. His life was good though misunderstood when life turned fast to fire and ash.

Little Miss Muffet found dead on her tuffet

Little Miss Muffet was found next to her tuffet with massive spider bites on her face and hands. Police believe she inadvertently sat on a nest of spiders and was unable to escape the attack. Her mother warned her to watch where she sat, but Miss Muffet ignored her.

The mystery to know was that where the spiders came from. It was in an unlikely place far from the willow tree she used to sit beneath. The faint laughter of children was heard by a traveller at the same time Miss Muffett cried out in pain. The Traveller looked round at the time, but saw no one. Later, when he read the morning newspapers about the incident did he come forward with what he heard.

Police are still investigating.

Big Bad Wolf arrested again

Just after being paroled from prison for the Three Pig Affair, Big Bad Wolf was arrested for murder at the Baconfest Festival. The well-known story that he was captured in a pot by the third pig was worthy of legend, but less than the truth. Big Bad Wolf was scalded terribly, but escaped through a side window before being captured by police only a mile away. The known serial killer of pigs will probably get life in prison.

An early investigation beforehand gave the police leads to other swine fatalities. Wolf has been searched after for the last few months and the police were sure that they had finally caught their killer.

Little Jack Horner not a good boy

Little Jack Horner arrested for stealing plum pies and repeating over and over again: "What a good boy am I" Judge called him a bad boy and sentenced him to be placed in a mental institution for observation.

His mother insisted it was a harmless obsession until it was proven Little Jack was in possession of hallucinate drugs. Little Jack was evaluated and found to be at a loss of his surroundings. He is still under observation at Manster State Hospital. His mother said that all he did all day was sit in a corner.

Woman who lived in shoe arrested for child trafficking

The woman who lived in a shoe had so many children that neighbors finally complained about the chaos of children running hither and yon. They, also, complained about the noise, but it was the shoelaces that lay across their property which finally brought the police in. The children kept untying the shoelaces as a joke, but no one else saw the humor. The neighbors were tired of tripping face first in the dirt.

When the police came to investigate, they found the shoe was dirty and unkempt smelling like old socks. Further investigation along with a warrant led to the old woman involved with child porn and trafficking over state lines. The police found eight children living in squalor in a small room beneath the shoelaces and another fourteen in the heel of the shoe.

    Upon searching the grounds they found ten makeshift graves just fifty feet from the shoe next to the garden. The old woman was arrested and charged with various counts of child endangerment, kidnapping, illegal porn and child trafficking. She was believed to be a fugitive that used to have a meth lab under the hill in another county. Before that she illegally immigrated from Europe leaving a host of children behind. She is now serving life imprisonment. Most of the children were identified and returned to their families. The others were put in foster homes.

    Through due diligence it was verified that the old woman was wanted in many towns for illegal activities, but still only the story of some woman under the hill will be told later.

Red Riding Hood Mystery

Many stories concerning Little Red Riding Hood abound. Some have the Woodsman saving her with an axe and others with a gun. The fact remains that the Woodsman saved Red and she was witness to the killing of her grandmother as well as the wolf hacked to death by the Woodsman. But there were events that changed the impressionable Red for life. Such a traumatic experience resulted in nightmares and sleepless nights. Red suffered in school and eventually dropped out.

The year following Red's narrow escape from the wolf only caused problems with her family. One day the police were called to Red's house when her parents mysteriously disappeared. The surrounding woods were searched and the house combed for clues, but no foul play was found. Her parents were never found and eventually lost to memory.

Later the court ordered Red into an orphanage where she stayed quietly for two years. Red's real name was Lizzy and one day a couple came looking to adopt the child. Mr. and Mrs. Borden seemed to be ideal parents and were allowed to take Lizzy home to Fall River, Massachusetts.

The Disappearance of Goldilocks

    Familiar story about Goldilocks except why she was wandering around Bear Woods by herself. What we weren't told was Goldilocks ran away from her parents and had been breaking into various homes throughout the forest. The Fox and Hedgehog family reported break-ins where food and a scarf were stolen. The Three Bears found her in the baby bear's bed after gorging herself with their porridge. The three bears were surprised to see her there and made themselves known. However she was able to escape into the forest through the back window.

    Now the mystery. Goldilocks was not seen again by anyone. Left behind was one lone shoe in the mud below the window she jumped out of when she ran from the three bears. Police and family searched for days to find Goldilocks and finally gave up. The thought was that she left the forest towards the big city. Ten years later a body was found on the shore of Bear Lake. The skeleton wore one lone shoe and it was presumed to be that of Goldilocks. No evidence was found connecting her to the three bears except the verbal evidence of the three bears. Whether they had something to do with her disappearance was never proven, yet was noted that none of them worked for a living. They never seemed to want for food or clothing so other things could be at work.

    Speculation was that she tried to swim to the other side of Bear Lake and drowned. Perhaps she had too much porridge and cramped up as she swam. Another theory was that the three bears followed her forcing her into the water and she was unable to swim.

    No matter the reason, Goldilocks now resided in the family cemetery along with an uncle and grandmother. Every Christmas a bouquet of flowers was found on her gravestone.

The Murder of Cock Robin

There is little doubt that Cock Robin was murdered by the Sparrow. What is not known is that Cock Robin was a loan shark and the Sparrow was a hit man hired by a variety of characters that owed Cock Robin money. How easily eyewitnesses and volunteers came to bury the criminal begs the question, why? Why bury him so quickly unless there were other crimes that surrounded the death of Cock Robin?

The Beetle was heard saying to the Fly: "Let's get rid of this bloodsucker!" It was not clear whether or not it was said before or after the murder. The Sparrow admitted killing Cock Robin with a bow and arrow yet has since left the forest to who knows where. It was believed that the sparrow was hired to kill Cock Robin.

Let's take each one of those involved one at a time. The eyewitness the Fly owed Cock Robin the most. The Beetle was just a blood ghoul who caught Cock Robin's blood for some unknown ritual. How could the fish make his shroud since it had no hands. Just plain disturbing.

The owl was the quickest to dig his grave even before the body was cold. The Rook was a shyster that never was ordained as a parson, but expected a fee to speak over Cock Robin's grave. The Lark could care less and asked for a large sum to be the clerk. The Dove was a chronic mourner and the girlfriend of Cock Robin.

Wren, Cock and Hen had to be slowed down trying to keep the coroner from the inspecting the body. Was there a drug connection that the police could not find? Bull happily rang the bell and was already drunk not knowing was going on. He was arrested for a drunk and disorderly charge, but it was only to allow the bull to sleep it off.

All the birds of the air cried when hearing the news. Of course, they were tears of joy since they owed him money, too. All lived happily after knowing that their debts were erased.

The police said it will take months, maybe a year to sort everything out.

Little Boy Blue

Little Boy Blue was a sad story about a little boy who presumably fell asleep while "the sheep were in the meadow and the cows in the corn." Those around him were afraid to wake him thinking he would cry if he saw what the animals were doing. However, it was two hours later when they discovered that there was pitchfork in the haystack he lay down on. The prongs had entered his back and pierced his heart. Sadly, he lay dead all that time. The family as well as the townspeople came from far and wide to bury the unfortunate child.

News update: An assassination plot was discovered against Prince charming and Cinderella. Cinderella's step sisters were arrested for planning to kill the unsuspecting couple just after their wedding. An anonymous call foiled the plot and the wedding continued as planned. Cinderella was not surprised but disappointed when she was told.

The old woman who lived under the hill

The story goes that the old woman who lived under the hill shut herself off from the rest of the world. The townspeople had left her alone because she kept mice and rats for pets. The Miller, who was her most vocal critic, spent many nights in the local tavern mocking the old woman with stories concerning her possible death. He joked that no one would have to dig her grave, but just lock her door. The old woman got wind of the stories and was aggravated so much she sent a mouse in a bag to the mill.

    The Miller did not have the heart to harm a mouse, so the old woman next sent a rat which the Miller was terrified of and bashed it with a hammer. Within the week the whole mill was struck down with the plague which killed the Millerand four other workers. The mill was shut down and thirty other employees were unemployed.

When the police came and told her what happened knowing that there was a conflict between them, she smiled. Later, the old woman disappeared and not heard from again.

News Update

Little Jack Horner who sat in the corner found dead at Manster State Hospital in his padded cell. As you remember, Little Jack Horner was a serial pie plunger stealing plums and continually saying over and over again "What a good boy am I". No foul play suspected as a nurse found the body sitting quietly with both thumbs up. Charges might be pending since his body was not found for hours. The nurse was disciplined, but not charged.

Old Mother Niddity Nod

Old Mother Niddity Nod started out for the Stoken Church Fair. Father Peter met her half way there. Why was this so important? The gossip was that Niddity Nod was a bootlegger where many became sick at last year's fair. Father Peter, though a fair man, wanted her to go home. There was a heated argument which led to Father Peter's disappearance. Whether he was killed or just ran away no one knows.

No body was found and Father Peter never sent word where he went. Niddity Nod did make it to the fair with her wondrous magic elixir and sold every bottle. Few seemed to care what happened to Father Peter and no one really searched for him. He was replaced by Father John of Warrensville. Niddity Nod was arrested years later for illegal stills and lack of permits to sell her elixir. It was said Father Peter neglected his church and took over her lucrative business.

"My dear, do you know,

How a long time ago

Two little children

Whose names I don't know

Were stolen away

On a fine summer's day

And left in a wood,

As I've heard people say."

    The Annotated Mother Goose, 1967

         p. 148-49

  The children were left by an unknown kidnapper without food or water. They supposedly laid down and died without even trying to find their way out of the woods. Months later their bodies were found with arms around each other. They were supposedly just babes in the woods, but who would do such a cruel thing?

Hanzel and Gretel were lost a second time after the witch and candy cottage incident. They were never found either, but the time line didn't match to those who were looking for them. This had been a long and terrible mystery investigation.

Other children were lost in the same wood as many thought it was a serial killer. Some blamed the Mad Woman of Challot, others blamed the woman under the hill or perhaps the old woman who lived in a shoe. There still is an ongoing investigation though few clues concerning the deaths of these "babes in the woods" are few and far between.

Peter who ate pumpkins mystery

Peter the pumpkin eater was arrested after his first wife complained that he had her imprisoned in a pumpkin. Peter was arrested for kidnapping with deprivation of food and drink. If it wasn't for the fact she loved pumpkin she never would have escaped her makeshift prison. Peter claimed his first wife was unfaithful and needed her to stay home. The only thing that kept Peter from jail was that his wife was in good health albeit she had a yellow tinge to her skin from eating her way out. There was no evidence of abuse or harsh treatment so all charges were minor. His wife protested and hired a second lawyer who had a grudge against Peter charged him with a list of crimes that resonated to the judge.

He was accused of drug trafficking, animal cruelty, farming without a license, embezzlement and desertion. At the trial Peter was asked if he had read the law about the crimes he had committed. He said that he could neither read nor write at the time so should not be guilty of any crime. The Judge told him that "ignorance of the law was no excuse" and sentenced him five to twenty years.

Peter's first wife divorced him while he was imprisoned. A chance meeting of a woman while he tried to get a retrial that led a second marriage. His second wife faithfully visited him for the first three years, but left him in the fourth year for Johnny Appleseed.

    She claimed that any type of pumpkin whether spice, pie or pudding made her sick. So she decided not to wait for Peter to serve his sentence. As a parting gift she made Peter an apple pie.

Rumpelstiltskin, murder or suicide?

The Queen was present when she guessed Rumpy's name. Rumpy was the unaffectionate name the police gave to Rumplestiltskin. When she guessed his name, Rumpelstiltskin exclaimed the devil told her his name. In anger he stomped his right foot into the ground and in his fury seized his left foot splitting his body in two. How could that happen? We have only the Queen's account to go by.

The Queen demonstrated in the past her ability throwing axes at various targets. She led soldiers into battle with axe and shield. The police believed, but could not prove, that she herself cleaved Rumpelstiltskin in half. Since she was the Queen, the police had to believe her account.

    Now what led to this confrontation? The Queen said Rumpelstiltskin kidnapped a child. Yet no child was found. The police thought Rumpy was practicing medicine without a license. Rumors had him as an ugly recluse that robbed unwary travelers on the roads that led to the palace. At any rate, the Queen knows, but will not speak of it.

Old Mother Hubbard arrested for animal cruelty

There was no question about the crime of animal cruelty by Old Mother Hubbard. She claimed to go fetch a bone for her dog. However, it was alleged that since she found the dog dead after going shopping leaves investigators wondering why a few hours shopping would have resulted in the death of her dog. Autopsy revealed that the dog had not been fed for weeks except for traces of bone and parts of a chair.

She claimed that she went to get a coffin for the dog and have it buried. However when she returned the dog was laughing at her. It was an obvious case of psychological break with reality since the investigators saw the dog was clearly dead. Old Mother Hubbard struggled with officers claiming the dog was surely alive. An officer picked up the poor dog and held it in his arms to prove it was dead. She responded "He's still laughing at me!"

Old Mother Hubbard was thought to be ninety years old and may have suffered from dementia. No known relatives could be found to help explain he actions. She is now under care at Mallard's Sanatorium.

Pied Piper — Child Trafficking

The events of that day were confusing. The leaders of Hamlin refused to pay for the Piper's services and the children were led into a mountainside. No one has seen the children since. Till now there was no connection until the arrest of the old woman who lived in a shoe. Authorities had wondered where all the children came from and now after the capture of the Pied Piper everything has come to light. Once the Pied Piper gave up his musical pipe, he confessed to all the mysterious disappearances of children throughout the land.

The Pied Piper spent the rest of his life in jail whistling now and again to keep the rats out of his cell. Every once in a while he stood face against the wall waiting for a door to open so he could get out.

Mary, Mary

Mary, Mary was quite contrary when the police came with a search warrant for the many gardens she was cultivating. It was the private garden in her basement that interested the police the most. There they found marijuana plants growing under special lighting.

When confronted, Mary, Mary also known as Mary Jane and Mary "smoke" Anderson is now serving 5-10 years for possession.

Wee Willie Winkie

Wee Willie Winkie may have thought that what he was doing was innocent, but going through the town in a nightgown was not amusing to neighbors or local police. His nightly rounds disturbed a few children trying to sleep comfortably from nightmares and the Boogie Man. The police arrested him for trespassing and a public nuisance.

He escaped and fled to another town. No one bothered to chase him.

Alice

  Alice tried to convince her parents that she truly went to Wonderland. When she started withdrawal symptoms her parents called police. After hours of hearing Alice talking about a talking cat, growing large and small while following a white rabbit the counselors called in were convinced she had a bad LSD trip.

  Alice later had one additional hallucinogenic episode which she described walking through a mirror into a backwards dimensional world. Though her stories were vivid and fascinating, her counselors suggested Alice be put into psychological ward for observation.

Alice was released six months later only to join a rock band three years later which advocated the use of LSD. She was the star singer at some great farm musical event a year later. Eventually, she went mad and married who she thought was a white rabbit.

Macavity the Mystery Cat

Macavity the mystery cat was the Moriarity of the animal world. Macavity had a distinct description so everyone knew what he looked like, but not where he was. Macavity was a known jewel thief, international spy and accused of numerous crimes that though the police were on his trail he always disappeared. This was a peculiar case that those who were involved always were left scratching their heads.

One day Macavity entered the police station of Scotland Yard and with a smile surrendered and confessed his crimes. He was jailed while lawyers built their case. That night when the officers went to take him to state prison and reached his cell Macavity was not there.

Little Bo-Peep

Little Bo-Peep was arrested for cruelty to animals. She told police she didn't know why her sheep's tails were cut off. The police searched her home days later and found a bloody knife hidden in the back room. The tails of the sheep were also found buried a few feet from her home. She was given probabtion of three years to work at an animal shelter.

The Odd Circumstances of Tommy Green

Tommy Green was accused of killing a cat by one Johnny Stout. There were no witnesses who saw Tommy Green actually throw the cat down the well so he was released. However, a week later the body of Robin Redbreast was found in Tommy Green's back yard. An arrow from a crossbow was found protruding through the chest of Robin Redbreast. Again there were no witnesses to the event and Tommy was released.

Two years later the ostrich, a silly bird, was found dead from an arrow shot from a crossbow. Tommy Green was seen running from the scene with something in his hand. When questioned, Tommy denied everything. Again he was released from lack of evidence and a search of his home revealed no weapons at all.

One day a year later, word of a Jabberwocky roaming the woods intrigued Tommy Green. He made a big show of having a crossbow and vowing to take on the great beast. A loud thrashing and crashing was heard as most the town came out to see what was happening. The noise pierced the air for a long time before a deafening silence enveloped the crowd that formed.

The ground shook under the townspeople feet as they filled with dread. The trees parted as the Jabberwocky stood a few feet from them with a crossbow in its teeth. With a smile it spat out the crossbow, turned and walked away. Tommy Green was never seen again. No one looked for Tommy and hoped they would never see him again.

Wee Willie Winkie's Wild Night

Running upstairs and downstairs throughout another town in a nightgown, Wee Willie Winkie, a vertically challenged man was arrested as a peeping tom. His incessant rapping on windows was disconcerting, but shouting through the lock "Are the children in their beds?" scared the children in the town.

Mrs. Artwould was the most disturbed since she was just getting out of her bath. Obviously, Wee Willie never learned his lesson and was arrested by the local police.

Wee Willie Winkie was brought to Hayfield Psychological Center for observation, but soon ran away in his nightgown and never seen again.

Wynken, Blynken and Nod

Drug Officials broke into the home of three fisherman Wynken, Blynken and Nod that neighbors claimed was an LSD house run by a Mr. Leary. The owner denied responsibility for those who visited his house. Mr. Leary protested that his three roomers did what they liked while staying there.

What made the neighbors suspicious were that two teenagers spoke of a wooden shoe with the three fishermen, Wynken, Blynken and Nod rowing in circles. The teenagers mentioned a talking moon as well as fishing nets of gold and silver catching stars as fish.

It was obvious they were under the influence of LSD and arrested Mr. Leary for the corruption of minors and possession of illegal drugs. There was a meth lab found later in a back shed which added five years to Mr. Leary's sentence.

Wynken, Blynken and Nod were released as innocent bystanders after drug tests proved negative.

The Balloon Man Bursts His Bubble

The Balloon Man was arrested today for a drug related crime concerning his balloons. Children were found at the market place acting silly and dazed after inhaling helium and an unidentified smoke like marijuana found inside. Though the Balloon Man released all his balloons when police arrived, the children tested positive for drugs.

The Balloon Man had been part of the market business area for five years with no prior incidents. The investigation continues to see if others are involved.

Within a few days the police found that the Balloon Man was bankrupt selling drugs to pay his debts.

The Cat And Cow Hallucinations

A very confusing tale that came from Mr. Leary after he was arrested happened while he was in the room. He talked about a cat playing a fiddle pointing out the feat as investigators were standing with him. They only saw a cat with its paw stuck in the strings of a guitar. The investigators found Mr. Leary's writing on a table that stated that he saw a cow jump over the moon. However there was a wheel of cheese on the ground. Did Mr. Leary jump over and back himself over the cheese?

He said the dog laughed when he saw what was going on, but one of his friends was sitting in a corner with a stupid smile on his face. The last vision was a dish running away with the spoon. Yet, on the floor was a broken dish and a spoon besides it as if they ended their lives in some suicidal pact.

    Mr. Leary was finally put away in an asylum still crying out that he saw visions and future events that no one wanted to hear about. The Judge heard what he said and decided Mr. Leary needed a lot of rest.

    Mr. Leary was released six months later when doctor's claimed he had kicked the habit and would not be a menace to society.

Little Periwinkie's Short Life

　　　Little Periwinkie

　　　Soft and slinkie

　　　Run over by a car

　　　Now is flat and stinky.

Jack Built a House Without Permission

Neighbors found Jack, a local contractor, working on a house. Upon entering the house they found half-eaten cheese, rats and undernourished cats. A dog was shackled in a room by itself. In the pasture behind the house was one lone cow mooing in despair.

A woman was found praying at a grave site while a homeless man shivered in the cold. Somehow a judge and a farmer got involved with it all when the farmer's horse entered the front door. Which when the farmer went to retrieve his horse found Jack sleeping on the floor.

Jack claimed it was his house, but could not produce a legal contract to prove it. The police arrested Jack for trespassing.

Mischievous Tom, the Tailor's Son

Tom, the tailor's son, was arrested for criminal mischief. Many of his father's customers complained about excessive itching after Tom's father cleaned their suits and pants.

No one knew what was going on until an undercover agent hid in the shop after it closed without telling Tom or his father. Around midnight, Tom came in and poured itching powder onto his father's press so that the powder would engrain itself into the clothes.

Tom was arrested, but received probation and forbidden to work with his father again.

Made in the USA
Charleston, SC
04 June 2015